CAPE TOWN
THE CITY AT A GLANCE

Signal Hill
The easiest piece of topography to ascend in
Cape Town. Drive or walk up for great views.
Since 1806, ships have set their chronometers
by the Noon Gun, which is still sounded today.

Green Point Common
Green Point Stadium, in the middle of the
Common, is being completely transformed
for the 2010 World Cup. Check on its progress
with a jog or stroll along the seafront.

City Hall
Built in 1905, City Hall's most memorable
moment came on 11 February 1990,
when Nelson Mandela made his first speech
after his release from prison on the balcony.
Darling Street, T 021 465 2029

Cape Town Railway Station
This classic 1950s station is complete with
original windows. Just don't visit at rush hour
when it heaves with commuters.
Adderley Street, T 021 449 2991

V&A Waterfront
Since redevelopment began in the late 1980s,
the Victoria and Alfred basins have changed
from derelict docks into a pristine and thriving
shopping, dining and tourism destination.

Castle of Good Hope
The 1679 castle is unimposing from
the outside, but is worth a visit for the
William Fehr collection of decorative arts.
Buitenkant Street, T 021 787 1249

Civic Centre
Councillors meet in the revamped podium
building, with its remarkable shuttlecock-like
roof, located beside the original concrete slab.
See p076

INTRODUCTION
THE CHANGING FACE OF THE URBAN SCENE

With a jaw-dropping location at the base of one of the world's most spectacular mountains, miles of Atlantic coast and acres of verdant winelands, it's possible to fall for Cape Town for its looks alone. Indeed, some accuse the city of being skin-deep, vacuous, full of pleasure-seekers sipping cocktails and surfing waves. In fact, they say, Cape Town isn't African at all. More of a pocket California. But that's part of the appeal. In the hedonistic heat of summer, Cape Town is South Africa's party central: it has the bars, the restaurants, the beaches, the beautiful people, the backdrop. And the locals – laid-back and welcoming – must have to pinch themselves: this film-set paradise is theirs every day. The tourists just pinch themselves at an exchange rate that makes excess so affordable. And with a Western European time zone at that.

A dozen or so years into South Africa's democracy, Cape Town is thriving, building, booming. There are boutique hotels, cottages and apartments to rival any in the world, and a growing design scene. Not that it doesn't have its problems. Apartheid is gone but inequality takes much longer to unravel. The township residents are still in the townships, the whites are still in their beachside pads. There is both optimism and edginess here, and safety is something to be sensible about. One thing's for sure, the city is changing fast. Take Cape Town's African-ness, mix in its otherness, shake or stir, and enjoy the unique cocktail for what it is.

ESSENTIAL INFO

FACTS, FIGURES AND USEFUL ADDRESSES

TOURIST OFFICE
107 Clock Tower
T 021 405 4500
www.tourismcapetown.co.za

TRANSPORT
Car hire
Allen's Car Hire
T 021 701 8844
African Welcome
T 021 762 4004
Helicopter
Civair
T 021 419 5182
Train
Metrorail
T 0800 656 463
Taxis
Sea Point Radio Taxis
T 021 434 4444
Marine Taxis
T 021 434 0434

EMERGENCY SERVICES
Ambulance
T 10 177
Police Tourist Assistance Unit
T 021 418 2852
Police Flying Squad
T 10 111
Late-night pharmacy (until 11pm)
Glengariff Clicks Pharmacy
2 Main Road, Sea Point
T 021 434 8622

CONSULATES
British Consulate General
Southern Life Centre, 8 Riebeeck Street
T 021 405 2400
US Consulate General
2 Reddam Avenue
T 021 702 7300

MONEY
American Express
11th Floor, Nedbank Building
57 Heerengracht
T 021 412 3000

POSTAL SERVICES
Post Office
Parliament Street
T 021 464 1700
Shipping
UPS
T 021 555 2745
www.ups.com

BOOKS
Sea-Mountain, Fire City: Living in Cape Town by Mike Nicol (Kwela Books)
Disgrace by JM Coetzee (Penguin)
South African Wines by Philip Van Zyl (John Platter)

WEBSITES
Art/Design
www.designindaba.com
Architecture
www.saia.org.za
Newspapers
www.capetimes.co.za

COST OF LIVING
Taxi from Cape Town International Airport to city centre
€31
Cappuccino
€1.45
Packet of cigarettes
€1.85
Daily newspaper
€0.45
Bottle of champagne
€72

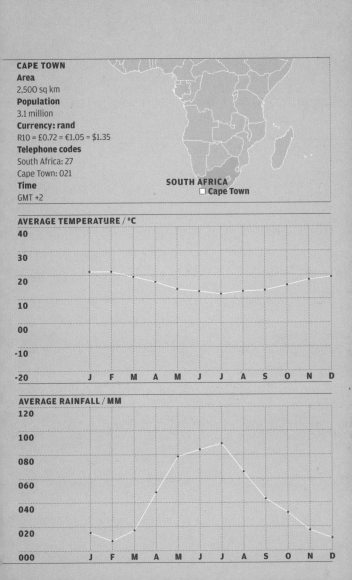

CAPE TOWN

Area
2,500 sq km

Population
3.1 million

Currency: rand
R10 = £0.72 = €1.05 = $1.35

Telephone codes
South Africa: 27
Cape Town: 021

Time
GMT +2

SOUTH AFRICA
☐ Cape Town

AVERAGE TEMPERATURE / °C

	J	F	M	A	M	J	J	A	S	O	N	D
40												
30												
20												
10												
00												
-10												
-20												

AVERAGE RAINFALL / MM

	J	F	M	A	M	J	J	A	S	O	N	D
120												
100												
080												
060												
040												
020												
000												

NEIGHBOURHOODS
THE AREAS YOU NEED TO KNOW AND WHY

To help you navigate the city, we've chosen the most interesting districts (see the map inside the back cover) and underlined featured venues in colour, according to their location (see below); those venues that are outside these areas are not coloured.

ATLANTIC SEABOARD
Super-suburbs Camps Bay and Clifton are littered with beautiful modernist homes and are, crucially, home to the city's sandy beaches. Accommodation here comes with sunsets straight out of central casting. Upmarket, if less vibey, Bantry Bay and Fresnaye have seafront but no beach, as does Sea Point, which is still a little edgy. All three areas are undergoing development.

GREEN POINT
The site of the new 68,000-seater football stadium for the 2010 World Cup, Green Point is set for massive change. The villagey De Waterkant, formerly a Cape Malay area, is already a gentrification success story; its Cape Quarter, a shopping and dining courtyard development, overflowed to create an area packed with fashionable interiors stores, cafés, restaurants, bars and clubs that is also the city's gay centre.

CITY CENTRE
Running through its heart, Long Street is a microcosm of the whole area. A nightlife hub with some of the city's best bars and restaurants, here the smart rubs shoulders with the shabby. To the west, don't miss Bo-Kaap, the Cape Malay quarter with its tiny, brightly coloured homes, and do stroll down Company's Garden, an unexpected haven. Also check out the redevelopment around the Greenmarket Square area, where old buildings are being converted into 3,500 apartments and retail space.

WATERFRONT
The V&A Waterfront (www.waterfront.co.za) is one of the city's proudest achievements – a safe and very successful retail and dining centre with multiplex cinemas and bars, and a working harbour full of luxury yachts – but also a slightly embarrassing place to be. Offering a kind of Disneyfied Victoriana, it could well be Covent-Garden-on-Sea. Skip the mall, be selective about the craft shops and go to Robben Island via the Mandela Gateway. There is an excellent information centre (T 021 405 4500) by the Clock Tower.

LOWER CITY CENTRE
Built on land reclaimed from the sea in the late 1930s, the Foreshore's existence is a triumph of engineering. It's a shame, then, that there's not a great deal to draw you into the area, as the Lower City Centre is mainly home to high-rises and motorway flyovers. Things looked up in 2003, with the opening of the Cape Town International Convention Centre, CTICC (1 Lower Long Street, T 021 410 5000), a world-class glass and steel conference facility.

CITY BOWL SUBURBS
Lining the lower slopes of Table Mountain (see p012) and Signal Hill, the suburbs of Vredehoek, Oranjezicht, Higgovale, Gardens and Tamboerskloof are among the city's most desirable addresses. The last three areas benefit from proximity to Kloof Street's upmarket cafés, restaurants and shops, and are home to the best boutique hotels.

LANDMARKS

THE SHAPE OF THE CITY SKYLINE

While elsewhere you might navigate by skyscrapers, bridges and parks, here, nothing is ever going to compete with the kilometre-high rock thrust up in the middle of the city. Perversely, it can be disorientating. From the ground, it's hard to get a handle on the fact that much of the city is always on the other side of one peak or another. In the City Bowl, nestled in the crook of Table Mountain (see p012) and Lion's Head, you can feel you are in a small town. Then you nip over Kloof Nek and the Atlantic Seaboard is revealed, with its beachside suburbs and a dozen more peaks, the Twelve Apostles, reaching along the coast. Scoot around the back of Table Mountain and miles more suburbs stretch all the way to False Bay.

Not that man hasn't made his mark. There's the monumental vacancy of District Six, a multiracial quarter that was bulldozed during apartheid and is only now being developed into affordable housing. The 1679 Castle of Good Hope (Buitenkant Street, T 021 787 1249), a low-lying pentagon, marks the former seafront before the Foreshore was reclaimed from the sea in the late 1930s. The area is now home to a collection of high-rises that define the CBD. Standing out, however, are structures that have become enduring symbols of the city almost in spite of themselves: the love-them or loathe-them Disa Park Towers (see p010), the time-warp Ritz Hotel (see p014) and the bombastic Rhodes Memorial (see p013). *For full addresses, see Resources.*

Disa Park Towers

Dubbed Tampon Towers by disgruntled locals, this unlikely trio of 17-storey 1960s apartment blocks is an eyesore to some and an icon to others. Built by Murray & Roberts on the lower slopes of Table Mountain, their height caused controversy and, to add insult to injury, the city's seasonal wind, the Southeaster, tends to blow the windows in.
Chelmsford Road, Vredehoek

Table Mountain

Obliging pilots cruise past Table Mountain as flights (sit on the left) arrive in Cape Town and it will dominate every view you have of the city during your stay. If the weather is clear (the mountain can be shrouded in cloud, the Table Cloth, for days on end), grab the opportunity and head up for the panorama from the top. You can hike up the 1,085m mountain (go well equipped and accompanied; an urban mountain is no safer than any other), but it takes just five minutes to reach the top in one of the 1997 Swiss-designed cable cars, each weighing 18 tonnes, which revolve as they go and carry up to 900 people an hour. There's a touristy café at the summit; far better to take something delicious from Melissa's deli (see p056) and a crisp Sauvignon Blanc. *T 021 424 8181, www.tablemountain.net*

Rhodes Memorial

The wonder of the Sir Herbert Baker and Sir Francis Macey-designed memorial to Cecil John Rhodes, the British diamond magnate, empire builder and prime minister of the Cape Colony from 1890-96, is that no one seems to mind its bombast. Inspired by a Greek temple, it sits, absurdly grandiose amid the greenery, zebras and wildebeest, on the Rondebosch slopes of Table Mountain, near the University of Cape Town. The rearing horse sculpture celebrates Rhodes' energy, while his bust is at the top of lion-flanked steps, inspired by the Avenue of Sphinxes in Karnak, Egypt. It's worth a stop (off the M3), largely for the view of the huge chunks of Cape Town that exist behind Table Mountain.

Ritz Hotel

A jaded 1970s tower with what looks like a spaceship on top, this is the least ritzy Ritz you are likely to find. It has been unkindly called the Pitz, but we don't feel the building should take the blame for that. Lurking off Main Road in Sea Point, it towers, almost embarrassed, above nondescript apartment buildings and shops, and is far and away the most interesting structure in the area. The spaceship, wonder of 1970s wonders, is actually a revolving restaurant on the 21st storey (T 021 439 6988). The bar is on the same floor but, thoughtlessly, not in the bit that goes round. So to go for a spin, you will have to order a prawn cocktail, which should nicely complete the whole time-warp experience.

Main Road/Camberwell Road, T 021 439 6010, www.africanskyhotels.com

HOTELS

WHERE TO STAY AND WHICH ROOMS TO BOOK

The film and fashion crowds have an ongoing love affair with oh-so photogenic Cape Town, and the accommodation that has sprung up to house them is wonderfully well equipped to deal with the demanding diva in all of us. There are two things to bear in mind. Location is important because, although it's not a sprawling city as such, Cape Town is divided into distinct neighbourhoods by its topography. If you're basing yourself on the Atlantic coast, for instance, it's tiresome to keep crossing back over Kloof Nek to get to the restaurants and shops of the City Bowl. Splitting your stay, with a central stint followed by a beach location, is one solution.

Secondly, consider just how important it is for you to be in a traditional hotel set-up. The most interesting places to stay are the ever-increasing raft of small villas, apartments and cottages, such as The Penthouse, Mutual Heights (opposite), Lion's View (see p036), On the Rocks (see p024) and The Village Lodge's cottages (49 Napier Street, T 021 421 1106). If you're a room-service addict, it's hard to look past the Mount Nelson Hotel (see p034), the old lady that is successfully reinventing herself as the Claridge's of Cape Town. In between, small guest houses and boutique hotels with a personal touch are flourishing, from the six-room Alta Bay (see p020) to the newer Manolo Sleep (33 Leeukloof Drive, T 021 426 2330), five luxurious suites nestled at the base of Signal Hill. *For full addresses and room rates, see Resources.*

The Penthouse, Mutual Heights

Robert Silke of Louis Karol Architects has created an amazing apartment in this art deco pile, formerly the Old Mutual Building, in very much an emerging, still slightly edgy 'hood. The 500 sq m space includes a study/home cinema and four bedrooms, all en suite, two of which share a high catwalk bridge across the lounge (above). The main bedroom has panoramic Table Mountain views; or watch the sun rise over the Helderberg Mountains from the breakfast terrace. We like that gourmet catering is standard; self-catering is an option, but you will be far too busy sipping martinis on the chaise longue (above), designed by Mutual Heights resident Haldane Martin. Request the chauffeur too. This option is all about glamour.
Parliament Street/Darling Street,
T 021 794 3140

Main entrance, Mutual Heights

Alta Bay

Some interesting artwork, a refreshingly understated approach to interiors – a beige palette leavened by the occasional use of meranti wood – and a sunbathing terrace lift this Higgovale boutique hotel (entrance hall, left) from the pack. With just seven suites, the emphasis is on personal service, while its lofty position on the slopes of Table Mountain, affording views of the city and ocean, adds to the sense that this is very much a retreat; in fact, the city centre is just a five-minute drive. The rooms each have their own outside space, either a wooden deck or a secluded patio; the Bay Room (above) has the biggest bathroom. Arrange a beauty treatment or massage followed by a glass of champagne on the upper terrace.
12 Invermark Crescent, T 021 487 8800, www.altabay.com

Metropole

If you really must be in the heart of the city's frenzied bar action, the 29-room Metropole offers modern boutique style in a renovated Victorian building, and is the kind of development that may eventually banish the area's remaining shabbiness. The communal areas, such as the all-white lobby and all-red M-Bar & Lounge (right, see p059), courtesy of interior designer François du Plessis, are high on glamour, while the functional rooms offer a more restful, pared-down aesthetic; some of the second-floor rooms have balconies and are a little quieter. Ask for Deluxe Suite 205 (above). Du Plessis was called back in 2006 to create the M-Café, a confection of chocolate and bronze with the obligatory ostrich-skin seating, which gives the M-Bar crowd a glossy day-time haunt in which to nurse their hangovers.
38 Long Street, T 021 424 7247,
www.metropolehotel.co.za

On the Rocks
This two-bedroom apartment is partially carved out of the cliff at Bantry Bay, with 10m of rock between the front door – suitably equipped with a salvaged ship's porthole – and the sea. You'll need a car to get to good restaurants and bars but the windows all across the front mean your seclusion comes with a superb view.
Seacliffe Road, T 021 424 0905, www.icape.co.za

Kensington Place

This eight-room hotel, located in smart, quiet Higgovale, has the intimate appeal of a bed and breakfast, and will delight romantics. There is an emphasis on comfort as well as elegance in the contemporary interiors, with original artwork from mostly African artists. Each of the rooms, such as Room 6 (above) is individually furnished and all have a private terrace with a view of the city, harbour and mountains (right). Room 8, with its own entrance, offers more privacy, and Room 7 has an almost-outdoor shower and sunken bath (there's just clear glass between you and the South African sunshine). The hotel is set in lush, quiet gardens with a plunge pool, and has its own bar and dining room. Complimentary and thoughtfully provided extras include iPod docking systems, laptops, Wi-Fi, Skype and Virgin Active gym membership. *38 Kensington Crescent, T 021 424 4744, www.kensingtonplace.co.za*

Hippo Boutique Hotel

This is economical, stripped-down hotel living at its best. The 20 well-finished en suite rooms (front-facing Standard Room, above) are large, sleek and modern, with king-size beds, cherry-wood floors, neat kitchen units and a computer-based entertainment system. Opt for one of the quieter rooms at the back – 105 is particularly spacious. The plunge pool is an unexpected bonus, the entrance delivers a refreshing dose of industrial chic, with bare brick and steel, and the staff are extremely friendly and helpful. There is no restaurant as such, but the location just off Kloof Street means there is a trio of eateries below that provide room service, including Greens on Park (T 021 422 4415), all sharing a terrace.
5-9 Park Road, T 021 423 2500, www.hippotique.co.za

The Twelve Apostles

This 70-room hotel offers splendid isolation and dramatic views of the ocean out front and the string of mountains after which it is named to the rear. It's a car journey to get anywhere, but you may be happy to be helicoptered in from the airport and stay for some serious R&R. The subterranean Sanctuary Spa has five treatment rooms, two outdoor mountain gazebos and a Rasul Chamber, where you can smother a friend in mud. Local treatments include Fynbos Exfoliation and a Buchu Wrap. There are also heated outdoor and rock pools and a private 16-seater cinema. The 46 rooms (sea-facing Superior Room, above) and 24 suites follow different themes, some rather frenetic, though Suite 101 has just the right dash of 1970s *Playboy* chic.
Victoria Road, Oudekraal, T 021 437 9000, www.12apostleshotel.com

Daddy Long Legs

Calling itself an art exhibition with space to sleep, this is the city's quirkiest hotel. Behind an elegant 1904 façade, each of the 13 rooms has been designed by a local artist. In The Freshroom, Karl Straub has made 2,500 rolls of Mentos mints part of the furniture, while the colour of the light can be changed to suit your mood. Antony Smith's The Photo Booth (overleaf), with its collage of 3,240 black and white portraits, is an excellent introduction to the locals. Saucier, and fabulously tongue-in-cheek, is Bert Pepler's 'hospital-chic' Emergency Room, with blood-red walls and a nurse's outfit. Rooms are small, but the experience is about novelty not luxury. The balcony of the bar (above) is a great spot for planning your assault on the eclectic nightlife below. *134 Long Street, T 021 422 3074, www.daddylonglegs.co.za*

The Photo Booth, Daddy Long Legs

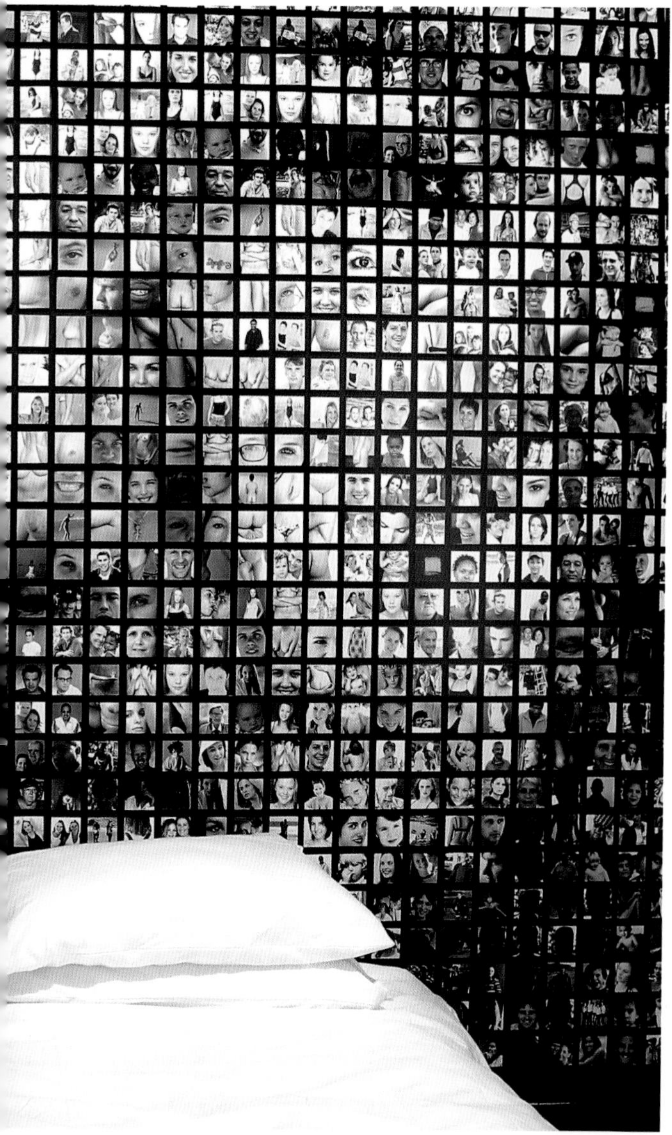

Mount Nelson Hotel

Celebrated local designer Graham Viney
has been successfully updating this grand
old hotel without throwing away its history.
It is still pink on the outside, but it's rather
less chintzy within. In 2006, balconies
and Italian-tiled bathrooms were added
to mountain-facing rooms on the fourth
floor, and next up is a state-of-the-art spa
within one of the city's oldest residential
buildings on nearby Faure Street. The six
Garden Cottages, with lavender up the path
to the veranda and roses round their own
front door, are adorable anomalies; inside,
the cottageyness does not preclude a
smart deco bathroom (right). Non-guests
should visit in summer for a very English
afternoon tea (T 021 483 1737), R125, on
the palm-lined lawns or a glass of bubbly
at its more contemporary institution, the
Planet Champagne Bar (see p065).
76 Orange Street, T 021 483 1000,
www.mountnelson.co.za

Lion's View

One of the first boutique Cape Town villas, designed by local architect Greg Wright, and still one of the best, Lion's View is a luxurious residence. Rent out either the five-bedroom Main House or the two-bedroom Penthouse, both of which come with a lounge (Penthouse, right), kitchen, pool, internet and all mod-cons. The Main House's Master Bedroom (overleaf), with its raised bath behind the bed and wall-to-wall view of the rim-flow pool and Camps Bay Beach beyond, comes with a telescope. The Penthouse has a terrace with a heated plunge pool (above), from where sunset-watchers are in for a treat; a tree silhouettes against the sky as if to order. Lion's View has a history as the star of many a fashion photo shoot. For guests, no request is too much trouble, whether you want a private chef or a helicopter tour.
4 First Crescent, T 021 438 1239, www.lionsview.co.za

24 HOURS

SEE THE BEST OF THE CITY IN JUST ONE DAY

Cape Town can please and tease you for a week and leave you wanting more. But if you really have only one day, focus on what the city does best; and without wishing to offend the culturally minded, that's food, wine, scenery, shopping and the beach.

On a clear day, the energetic might grab a pre-breakfast slice of scenery by climbing up Table Mountain, jogging at its base or along Green Point's seafront. Otherwise, make straight for a divine breakfast at Manna Epicure (opposite) on hip Kloof Street, then go shopping in the street's boutiques. Don't linger too long, as the next stop is a treat. The winelands surrounding Cape Town deliver phenomenal food and views within an hour's drive. Sample the best dining and mountain vistas at Tokara Restaurant (see p042).

Then make time to enjoy another of the city's USPs, the beach. We've opted for dramatic Llandudno (see p044), which is an excuse for a drive down the coast. If you have time, keep going and hug the made-for-car-ads curves of Chapman's Peak Drive. Later, it's back to Cape Town for some diamond shopping. Pick out a rock and have it cut to size at Prins & Prins (see p046). Kick off your evening with drinks at Café de Sud (107 Loop Street, T 021 422 0500) before dinner at Manolo (see p047). If you're still raring to go, hit Hemisphere (2 Riebeeck Street, T 021 421 0581), 31 floors up the ABSA Centre, where even the loo has a stunning view. *For full addresses, see Resources.*

09.00 Manna Epicure

At the upper end of Kloof Street, you will find Manna Epicure, where the delicious breakfasts and lunches are definitely from heaven (restaurant closed on Mondays). The quirky menu blends sweet and savoury in tasty combinations. Fennel, plum and raspberry salad with brie and shaved Belgian white chocolate is good for lunch, for instance, but we recommend coming here for breakfast, to try the scrambled eggs with coconut bread or the excellent eggs Benedict. A seat on the shaded terrace is the perfect spot to sit and study the beautiful young things of Tamboerskloof, while toying with your cute pink or blue espresso cup (the only things that aren't white). In the unlikely event you're still hungry, buy some of the fabulous home-baked bread to take away.

151 Kloof Street, T 021 426 2413

12.30 Tokara Wine Estate
Take a tour of this purpose-built winery
before having lunch at Tokara Restaurant
(closed Sundays and Mondays). Chef
Etienne Bonthuys' French-influenced
dishes are typified by his unusual
combinations; think grilled springbok
with a lobster sauce and mint oil.
Helshoogte Pass R310,
Stellenbosch, T 021 808 5959,
www.tokararestaurant.co.za

14.30 Llandudno
The city's best sunbathing options are the fashionable beaches of Clifton and Camps Bay, the latter with bars and restaurants, both only a 10-minute drive from the centre, while Oudekraal is available for private hire from 6pm (T 021 438 9555). But to really appreciate the wild coast, head 20km to Llandudno (pictured), a fabulous cove with huge, sculptural boulders at either end.

16.30 Prins & Prins

If diamonds are forever, you may as well get them right the first time. And, in South Africa, where they are the local stone, after all, bespoke doesn't necessarily mean going for broke. At Prins & Prins, you can choose a rough diamond or other stone and have it cut to your requirements while you watch. Experts will talk you through carats, colour and clarity and, if you wish, your gem can be set in jewellery designed to order by master goldsmiths. Whether or not you're buying, this 1752 building, one of Cape Town's earliest and boasting 18th-century wall paintings, is worth a visit.
Huguenot House, 66 Loop Street,
T 021 422 1090

21.30 Manolo

Local designer Kevin Engelbrecht has helped the Dutch owners create three distinct, intimate dining spaces in this 100-year-old villa. There's quite a scene in the garden in high season, and in 2006 the veranda was entirely glassed in, meaning your cocktail will these days remain unrippled even when Cape Town's Southeaster blows its worst. Relax with a Manolo Chill (vodka, 'bubbles' and lemon sorbet) at the underlit white marble bar before dinner – top chef Philip Alcock's menu is the sort of Afro-European mix that almost gives fusion a good name – and stay for a digestif in the raffish cigar lounge.
30 Kloof Street, T 021 422 4747, www.manolo.co.za

URBAN LIFE
CAFÉS, RESTAURANTS, BARS AND NIGHTCLUBS

It used to be impossible to eat or drink badly, or pay too much for sub-standard fare in Cape Town. Those days are over, but with care it's still possible for New Yorkers to be pleasantly surprised, Parisians less disappointed than usual and Londoners positively ecstatic about the quality/price relationship in the city's eateries.

Restaurants and bars in beachside areas like Camps Bay can get sloppy in high season, but the City Bowl places are reliable, and the cafés in upcoming, outlying areas such as Muizenberg and Kalk Bay are a revelation. Muizenberg might be rough around the edges, but as house prices have rocketed in the ocean-front 'hoods back in town, a new generation is moving further afield to colonise its Victorian eyesores facing the shore, and opening restaurants and bars. The winelands also deserve attention, with many wineries offering superb restaurants as well as tasting rooms, such as Tokara (see p042) and those in Franschhoek (see p102).

Cape Town is notoriously fickle; venues open to a frenzy of interest, can be the in-thing for six months and then disappear off the radar, usurped by a newer passion. We've selected a mixture of the city's long-term loves, such as 1970s time-warp La Perla (see p068), and newer stars like Birds Boutique Café (see p053), which is pioneering the fresh organic cause. In December and January, Cape Town turns into one big beach party, so book well ahead.
For full addresses, see Resources.

Newport Market & Deli

On a sunny morning, take a bracing walk along the Sea Point promenade to Mouille Point, watch the joggers, dog walkers, strolling lovers and the rolling Atlantic waves, and finish up with breakfast at this friendly and excellent deli, where locals come for weekend breakfasts and a read of the papers. Run by Capetonian husband and wife team Allan and Briony Schapiro, the Newport offers delicious smoothies and generous fruit/muesli/yogurt combos, home-baked cakes and biscuits, as well as lunches. You can also pick up a copy of Wallpaper* and browse various local design and interiors titles. Wakame (T 021 433 2377), a Pacific Rim restaurant upstairs, does good sushi and sunsets. *47 Beach Road, T 021 439 1538*

Harbour House
Anywhere else and this eaterie would be a tourist trap, but here, in Kalk Bay, it works as a modest temple to simply prepared seafood in a low-key and friendly setting. If you can't get a table, have a drink on the comfy sofas on the terrace. Downstairs, Polana (T 021 788 7162) is another fine seafood restaurant.
1st floor, Kalk Bay Harbour,
T 021 788 4133

Olympia Café and Deli

Of course, it shouldn't really matter that this seafront hangout attracts the best-looking crowd in the city, yet — call us shallow — it somehow does. It's almost impossible to secure a window seat for Sunday brunch and there's no booking, but it's really the only place in the city worth queueing for. The building could still be the bait and tackle shop it once was, the décor is nonchalant and the traffic rumbles past right outside. But it's for Olympia's excellent, freshly baked bread and pastries, good coffee and full eggy breakfasts, along with the Harbour House's lunches (see p050), that Capetonians flock to Kalk Bay at weekends. If you can't squeeze onto a table, take away a coffee and cinnamon twist to eat on the harbour-front.

134 Main Road, T 021 788 6396

Birds Boutique Café

Some of the most distinctive eateries in town are the small cafés that have sprung up offering fresh homemade breads, cakes and salads and good coffee. Birds is the best of the bunch, not least for its way with typography and unfussy modern interior – rough wooden trestle tables and cushioned plastic crates for seats act as makeshift chic. It's run by Namibian mother and daughter Mathilde and Heike Stegman, while another daughter, graphic designer Frauke, is behind the trademark bird silhouettes and crockery (available to buy). Initially a breakfast and lunch venue, Birds now holds special evenings on one Friday and Saturday a month, such as 'full-moon markets' promoting biodynamic produce, and organic bread and wine nights. *127 Bree Street, T 021 426 2534*

Vida e Caffé

The first and by far the best branch of the iconic South African coffee shop chain is located at the epicentre of the Kloof Street scene and is a perfect spot for breakfast. Grab an outside table, order one of the trademark paninis or a sublimely moist muffin (from classic blueberry to banana and pecan or apple and cinnamon) and marvel at Cape Town's *jeunesse dorée* going about its business.

Vida is packed on weekend mornings and has given Capetonians somewhere to go for informal weekday breakfast meetings. From outside, you'll see more than a smidgen of Table Mountain; indoors, the music is upbeat and the staff even more so, and far louder than the customers. This is the ultimate anti-Starbucks set-up.
Shop 1, Mooikloof Gardens, 34 Kloof Street, T 021 426 0627, www.vidaecaffe.co.za

95 Keerom

Chef Giorgio Nava's extension to Rhodes House is an exercise in pared-down excellence. Opt for a table in the upper dining room for light and space or go downstairs for intimacy. On offer is hearty, modern Italian cooking; trust the recommendations of Giorgio himself, who, with authentic Italian-accented aplomb, will come to your table to explain the daily specials, and special they are. Key ingredients unavailable locally are shipped in – buffalo mozzarella is flown from Naples every other day – fish is fresh daily and the inevitable African twist comes from dishes such as grilled black wildebeest with olive oil and rosemary. If that doesn't tempt you, try the rolled pork neck filled with ricotta and spinach, or there are eight kinds of carpaccio.
95 Keerom Street, T 021 422 0765

Melissa's

For a deli lunch, coffee and cake or gifts to take home, Melissa's is a Kloof Street institution and now has other branches, including one in Green Point (T 021 434 1719). At lunch, the only thing to stop you overloading at the buffet is the knowledge that you will be charged according to your plate's weight. That and the need to leave room for the malva pudding.
94 Kloof Street, T 021 424 5540

Royale Eatery

Tucked unobtrusively among the raft of wannabe NYC East Village bars and eateries in Long Street is this modest gem. It's the banquettes and burgers formula you've seen a thousand times before, but carried off with considerable élan. Choose from an inspired range of meaty and veggie burgers, such as Big Bird (a tasty ostrich and beetroot relish confection). The smoking section is comfier than the non-smoking and offers a prime table in the open window. Royale has opened an upstairs, shabby chic bar, The Waiting Room, with striking copper pendant lights and a couple of balconies from which to watch the comings and goings below over a Windhoek beer. If you can't bear not to see Table Mountain, there's a roof terrace on the third floor.
273 Long Street, T 021 422 4536

M-Bar & Lounge

François du Plessis' celebrated womb-red interior is definitely not for those who aren't prepared to let a little gaudy mock croc (and, naturally, ostrich) into their otherwise pared-down design aesthetic. However, the location in the Metropole hotel (see p022), the glitz and the good-looking crowd make this a fine place to kickstart your evening. Avoid the scrum on Fridays, unless you want to dance to the 'sexy lounge beats' of the unalluringly named DJ Tony Finger. Should it all get too much, or your small talk let you down, there are flat-screen TVs in the ladies'. *Metropole, 38 Long Street, T 021 424 7247, www.metropolehotel.co.za*

Capella

For a definitive taste of Cape Town opulence, head to Capella. No disrespect, but chef Scott Henry's African fusion menu isn't really what it's all about. However well-dressed the dishes and guests, neither can compete with the lavish interiors: the shapely ostrich-egg chandeliers, Swarovski crystals and kudu-hide stools, offset by 150-year-old carved Indonesian doors, are straight out of a photo shoot and, indeed, that's where they often feature. Don't wear your animal print, as you'll clash with the zebra banquette. Part of the successful Opium Group, Capella is the perfect precursor to post-dinner posing at nearby club Opium (T 021 425 4010), which offers chocolate chilli martinis and every kind of house music.
21 Somerset Road, T 021 425 0439, www.capellarestaurant.co.za

Onewaterfront
If you can see past the bad acoustics
and corporate décor of the cavernous
room, chef Bruce Robertson's cooking
is among the best in the city. Within
the Cape Grace Hotel, this restaurant
is a gem. Ask for a corner table looking
out at Table Mountain and enjoy dishes
such as shucked oysters and coriander
kingklip with parmentier potatoes.
West Quay Road, T 021 418 0520

Tank

Relaxed Italian deli and restaurant Andiamo (T 021 421 3687) and the Nose Restaurant and Wine Bar (T 021 425 2200) are ideal if you want to sit outside in the Cape Quarter courtyard and people watch. But for something a bit more fancy, Tank is a slick sushi restaurant, boasting a 25,000-litre fish tank, smart modern interiors and a vibey atmosphere. The chef, Arata Koga, is rated as the seventh sushi master in the world. The Pacific Rim menu extends to venison, chicken, duck and beef, as well as seafood, and includes tempura specialities. There's no view to speak of, but the open kitchen means that you can position yourself to watch the master at work as he wields his knife at the counter.

Cape Quarter, 72 Waterkant Street, T 021 419 0007, www.the-tank.co.za

Planet Champagne Bar

The champagne and cocktail bar of the Mount Nelson Hotel (see p034), given a modern design by Graham Viney in 2004, fast became an early evening destination for *le tout* Cape Town and is at the heart of the hotel's rebirth. It's almost always packed and remains so until late, so it's worth reserving a table. Or arrive early (it opens at 5pm, and 3pm on Fridays, making it a natural progression

from the hotel's afternoon tea, T 021 483 1737), position yourself at the bar and try a South African sparkling wine, such as Pierre Jourdan. The ceiling's orrery and Milky Way fibre-optic lights don't provide the only star gazing; the hip young crowd includes models and pop stars as well as lithe locals. It gets noisy; come to see and be seen, rather than for an intimate chat. *76 Orange Street, T 021 483 1000*

Forty Ate

This is a restaurant, lounge, cigar bar and art gallery in one, arranged over three floors of a listed 19th-century building by its Belgian owners, art dealer and interiors consultant Jörg Hasenbach and restaurateur Serge de Block. Forty Ate should take care of a whole evening's entertainment. Start at the top in the airy gallery, featuring 20th-century and contemporary art. Back on the ground floor, perch on a Haldane Martin-designed 'Weightless' stool at the marble bar and sip a cocktail before heading to the first-floor dining room and perusing chef Mark Hoberman's menu. His deconstructed dishes mean you might find yourself with a syringe, injecting a baked tomato with basil sauce, or assembling your own bouillabaisse. If it's all too taxing, retreat to the velvet sofas of the leather-padded cigar lounge downstairs to puff away.
48 Hout Street, T 021 422 2270

La Perla
The food's not really the thing at this Sea Point institution. There's an afternoon drinking crowd straight out of *The Sopranos*, and if the furniture looks like it hasn't changed since the 1970s, that's because it hasn't. There's a delightfully den-like bar inside, but if want to eat, get a table on the terrace, take in the view, and don't mind the rusting chrome.
Beach Road, Sea Point, T 021 439 9538

INSIDER'S GUIDE

BRONWYN DAVIES, FASHION STYLIST

A resident of Fresnaye on the Atlantic Seaboard, fashion stylist Bronwyn Davies does a lot of her shopping in De Waterkant. 'Hand (see p082) is a hair salon that also sells clothes and jewellery,' she says, 'and I often look around Jo Carlin (Shop 1, Jarvis House, Jarvis Street, T 021 421 6657) for the dresses.' La Petite Tarte (Shop A11, Cape Quarter, Dixon Street, T 021 425 9077) takes care of afternoon tea and a French pastry. On Sundays, a favourite lunch is musselcracker fish, a local delicacy, which she says is best at Codfather seafood and sushi restaurant in Camps Bay (37 The Drive, T 021 438 0782). 'Get there early before they sell out,' advises Davies. For a special occasion, she goes to Haiku (33 Church Street, T 021 424 7000) for its innovative Asian tapas.

Like most residents, Davies likes to spend the afternoon on the beach. 'The choice of where to go is a complete social nightmare. Conventional wisdom is that the fourth Clifton beach is the best, but my tip is Glen Beach. It's not as glamorous, but it's friendly and unpretentious, like the best bits of the city. Afterwards, I'd head for a drink at Cape to Cuba (Main Road, T 021 788 1566), which is right on the water's edge in Kalk Bay.' As a treat, Davies and her partner hire out the 16-seat cinema at The Twelve Apostles hotel (see p030) and have drinks at its Leopard Room Lounge and Bar, which has spectacular views of the ocean.

For full addresses, see Resources.

ARCHITOUR

A GUIDE TO CAPE TOWN'S ICONIC BUILDINGS

Fans of modernist architecture should visit the sleek residences that tumble down the slopes of the upmarket beachside suburbs Camps Bay and Clifton, or make for the newer wineries, such as Dornier Wines (Blaauwklippen Road, T 021 880 0557), that now punctuate the gabled, thatch-roofed Cape Dutch pads around Franschhoek (see p102) and Stellenbosch (see p042). Cape Town's 1950s railway station will please the nostalgic, but don't go at rush hour. There's something for brutalists too, as the apartheid regime, better known for bulldozing than building, saw an appeal in robust concrete architecture, such as the Civic Centre (see p076).

The city is in the midst of a building and refurbishment frenzy. Of most interest is the city-centre revival, started by Louis Karol's transformation of the art deco Old Mutual Building (see p017) into lofts. However, in a city bearing the imprint of its Dutch and British colonisers – the latter bringing imperial pomp with buildings such as 1905's City Hall (Darling Street, T 021 465 2029) and, along the way, adding the wrought-iron railings that so define Long Street – and last century's town-planning of segregation, when township 'matchbox' houses and shanty-town shacks took their place in the vernacular, it's no surprise that, today, the best architecture is often more about a thoughtfully designed township school or arts centre (see p078) or affordable housing than it is about statement-making. *For full addresses, see Resources.*

Taal Monument

Architect Jan van Wijk's remarkable 1975 tribute to South Africa's unique hybrid language – a mixture of Dutch, French, English, Malay, German and indigenous languages, all of them symbolically recognised in the monument's granite columns – is, if nothing else, a great picnic spot on the way to the winelands of Franschhoek (see p102) and Stellenbosch. These days, Afrikaans is the country's third most widely spoken language (behind Zulu and Xhosa, ahead of English) out of 11. However, when the monument was built, Afrikaans was heavily associated with apartheid; the government policy of making it the only language of instruction in schools led directly to the Soweto uprising of 1976. In Cape Town alone, 128 people were killed as a result.
Paarl Mountain

Baxter Theatre Centre
This 1977 brick masterpiece is the
defining work of late Capetonian Jack
Barnett. With a concert hall and theatre,
it was known for opening its doors to
all during segregation. The exterior is
imposing with intricate touches. The
recessed orange dome lights above
the entrance are a taste of the dozens
more that line the ceiling inside.
Main Road, Rondebosch, T 021 685 7880

Civic Centre

A large slab of apartheid-era brutalism, Naudé, Pappendorff, Van der Merwe and Meiring's 1978 Civic Centre, a concrete and glass tower, 98m tall and twice as long, with a lower podium building in front of it, wasn't the most obvious choice for the home of Cape Town's newly unified city government (Unicity) in late 2000. But the podium was expertly renovated by KrugerRoos architects who, by adding an upper level, created a structure that is all about openness and light, with glass used wherever possible to underline the transparency of council business. The inverted steel cone that forms the roof of the council chamber (right) symbolises a fresh start, but is also a wind disperser and shading device, as well as contributing to the acoustics and changing colour with the weather. It is not, as some locals first thought, scaffolding that got left behind.
12 Hertzog Boulevard, T 021 400 3032

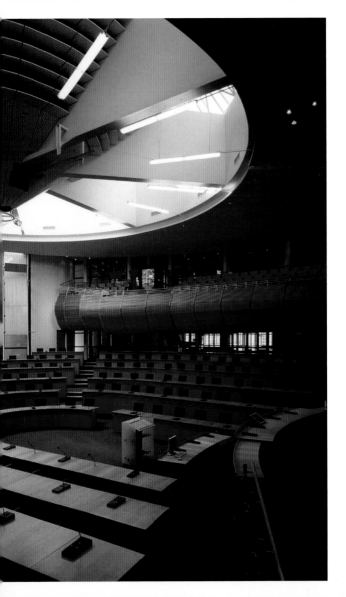

Guga S'Thebe Arts & Culture Centre

In Langa, Cape Town's oldest township established in 1923, the Guga S'Thebe Arts & Culture Centre was designed and built in consultation with the local community whom it would serve. The result is an eclectic but distinctly African piece of architecture that contrasts with anything else you are likely to see in the city centre and suburbs. The buildings are designed to resemble a traditional settlement and the golden cone is a contemporary take on an African hut. Local artists and schoolchildren were invited to design murals for the building's walls. Commissioned by a Cape Town tourist organisation, it was realised by CS Studio Architects' Carin Smuts. A venue for teaching arts and crafts, it also hosts exhibitions and houses a business centre. *Washington Street, Langa, T 021 695 3493*

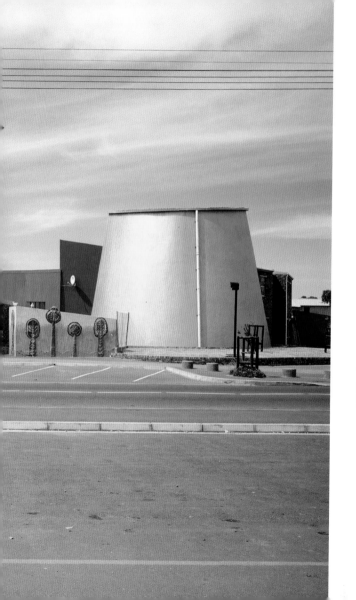

SHOPPING
THE BEST RETAIL THERAPY AND WHAT TO BUY

Kloof Street, with its tony boutiques, and De Waterkant, with trendy interiors stores spilling out beyond the Cape Quarter, are moochers' paradises, where you'll find the best of the city's shopping. Expect small, unassuming stores and cute one-offs. While plenty of shops stock the work of Cape Town designers, such as Heath Nash (see po86), make time to investigate the designers' own studios, where you can also commission something. You'll find several of these in Woodstock, such as at the Old Biscuit Mill; a warehouse converted into workshop space, it also hosts the hip Neighbour Goods Market on Saturdays (373-375 Albert Road, T 021 448 1438).

Crafts are a good Cape Town buy. Clementina's Ceramics in Kalk Bay (20 Main Road, T 021 788 8717) has the best choice, from her earthy-toned ceramics to the laser-cut metal Christmas trees by TinTown (T 021 426 2226). Fashion is less well represented. Klûk (Main Road/Upper Portswood Road, T 083 377 7780) offers a flavour of South African couture, while edgier local designers are available at stores such as MeMeMe (117a Long Street, T 021 424 0001) and Hand (see po82). For glamour, try a vintage chandelier from Delos (138-140 Buitengragt Street, T 021 422 0334); they're imported, but the local restoration makes them a Capetonian bargain. If you can't carry everything back, buy an art deco pad to put it all in at Engel & Völkers (103 Kloof Street, T 021 426 4848). *For full addresses, see Resources.*

Michael Stevenson Gallery

If you're browsing in De Waterkant, seek out Michael Stevenson's bright, white, custom-designed space (look for Hill House, the building's name, as the gallery is unmarked at the main entrance). We took a shine to artist Doreen Southwood, whose best work, such as 'The Swimmer' (above), exposes the underbelly of her white, middle-class Afrikaans upbringing. The gallery also shows some interesting photographers, such as Pieter Hugo, who won the World Press Photo 2006 portrait competition with 'Mallam Galadima Ahamadu with Jamis, Nigeria, 2005', a striking image of a man with a hyena on a leash; and David Goldblatt, who has been documenting the political landscape in South Africa for 50 years. There's a good selection of art books and catalogues too. *Hill House, De Smidt Street, T 021 421 2575*

Hand

Typical of gentrified De Waterkant's inhabitants are Hélène Bull, a fashion designer, and hair stylist Michael Scott. Pooling their talents and showing an innovative approach to interiors, they have turned this first-floor space into an offbeat hair and beauty salon-cum-fashion and jewellery store, with a coffee area. At the three hand-designed cutting stations, the seats are old Italian office chairs and the lights are on Chopper bike handles, while the white superwood tables and chairs have ornate leg outlines vinyled on. 'Hand' stands for 'Have A Nice Day', but also references the hand-picked products; while they're not all handmade, they're not mass-produced and many are local, such as Philippa Green's bracelets (see p084), and earrings by Hannah Lurie. *28 Hudson Street, T 021 425 9912*

Olive Green Cat

Philippa Green's beautiful bracelets make the perfect holiday gift. Rather than hunt down the limited range in some of the city's smaller boutiques, give her a call and check out her Kloof Street workspace and shop named Olive Green Cat, especially if you would like to commission something a little special. She's best known for her sleek, patterned perspex cuffs (above, with stitched nylon), R1,200, but she also works with wood and silver and produces interesting rings and elegant pendants. Her latest range, 'SITU', created with designer Ida-Elsje, features diamonds and resin. Green, who studied fine art at Durban Technikon before turning to jewellery making, is one of the city's best known and most successful designers.
79 Kloof Street, T 082 466 8571

Okha

Cape Town has not got a reputation as the first port of call for slick modern furniture, but many places now cleverly utilise local materials. Designer Haldane Martin (www.haldanemartin.co.za) has used the quintessential African wood, zebrano, in a plywood veneer to construct this elegant chair (above), R3,700, also, inevitably, available with a springbok-hide seat. It's part of his 'Weightless' range, which features distinctive lightweight stainless-steel frames inspired by African wirework sculptures, and includes stools, tables and an ergonomic dining chair. Find Martin's work at Okha, one of Cape Town's first contemporary furniture stores. Linked to architects Antoni Associates, its locally produced designs furnish many of the city's most desirable residences.
186 Loop Street, T 021 424 9706

Heath Nash

One of the young stars of South African design, Heath Nash was originally a sculpture major at Cape Town's Michaelis School of Fine Art. He is passionate about presenting updated versions of traditional local handicrafts and does some amazing things with recycled plastic. His 'Flower Ball' lampshades are a hit, but if they seem too evocative of floral swimming caps from the 1970s, he has plenty more understated lighting and screen designs, as well as his personal favourite: the wire 'Soccer' bowl (right), R1,200-1,600. Conran now stocks some of Nash's work and he has signed up with producer Artecnica, which is all the more reason to order something no one else will have direct from his modest showroom in down-at-heel Woodstock.

2 Mountain Road, T 021 447 5757/082 403 6958, www.incapetown.com/heathnash

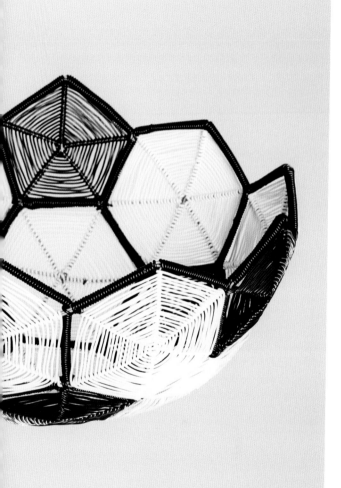

SPORTS AND SPAS
WORK OUT, CHILL OUT OR JUST WATCH

There is plenty to please thrill-seekers in this city. The mountains, apart from being good to climb (Mountain Club of South Africa, T 021 465 3412), are good for throwing yourself off. Abseil from Table Mountain (Abseil Africa, T 021 424 4760), paraglide off Signal Hill or Lion's Head, or try extreme mountain biking (Downhill Adventures, T 021 422 0388). Take to the water in a 50ft sloop (Waterfront Boat Company, T 021 418 5806), go sea kayaking (PaddleYak, T 021 790 5611), fishing (Cape Sea Safaris, T 021 422 4611) or cage diving with Great Whites (Sharklady Adventures, T 028 312 3287). Or take off in a supersonic ex-military jet (Thunder City, T 021 934 8007). The best gym is Virgin Active (Wembley Square, McKenzie Road/Wesley Street, T 021 462 6239), but more in tune with the outdoor vibe is to swim at Sea Point Pavilion (see p090), jog along the seafront, play ball games on Clifton's beaches or surf at Muizenberg (see p094).

As for spectator sports, Cape Town has three loves – rugby, cricket and football, which has the city talking with the approach of the 2010 World Cup in South Africa. The city's matches will be held at the soon-to-be-revamped Green Point Stadium, but you can catch local football team Ajax (www.ajaxct.com) at Athlone Stadium. However, watch a rugby match from the standing section at Newlands Stadium (11 Boundary Road, T 021 659 4600) and you will learn what really arouses passion in the South African male. *For full addresses, see Resources.*

Newlands Cricket Ground

As with just about every Cape Town venue, the setting makes it. For all the English village-green gentility that's evoked by a well-groomed pitch and cricket whites, there's nothing like the thrusting presence of Devil's Peak looming above to lend a sense of drama to the proceedings, and create what locals love to claim is the most picturesque cricket stadium in the world. Not to be confused with the nearby Newlands Stadium, where the sports of choice are rugby and football, recent upgrading of the cricket ground, which hosted its first game back in 1888, has not pleased everyone, aesthetically at least. However, it's the perfect spot in which to while away an afternoon watching either the local team, Cape Cobras, or an international game if you're very lucky. *146 Campground Road, T 021 657 2003*

Sea Point Pavilion

Cape Town has lots of sea but little of it
is swim-friendly. For serious exercise or
to dip your toe in for the sake of the
venue, go to Sea Point Pavilion (open
7am-7pm in summer; 8.30am-5pm in
winter). Built 50 years ago and blissfully
unchanged, there are four saltwater
pools, one of which is Olympic-sized,
all slightly warmer than the sea.
Beach Road, T 021 434 3341

Altira Spa

Tempted as we are by the thought of an outdoor massage in the mountain gazebos at the Twelve Apostles Sanctuary Spa (see p030), pampering is one luxury we prefer to enjoy indoors; where we feel less foolish in a fluffy gown and where there is no danger of a fly in our face pack. But there's no need to sacrifice the view. On the 19th floor of the Arabella Sheraton Grand Hotel, the Altira Spa's heated lap pool overlooks the harbour. Follow a dip with a hot stone massage and relax on a heated water bed, before lunch at the Towers Club Restaurant (T 021 412 8082), which offers yet more wraparound views. *Arabella Sheraton Grand Hotel, Convention Square, Lower Long Street, T 021 412 8200, www.altiraspa.com*

Muizenburg

Both genuine surf types and wannabes should test Cape Town's waters. At Muizenberg, brightly painted beach huts flake in the sun and, in the 1920s, even Agatha Christie caught some waves off the sandy beach. Equipment hire and lessons can be arranged at Gary's Surf School (T 021 788 9839). Then head to Cape Point via even more cute beach huts at St James (pictured).

ESCAPES

WHERE TO GO IF YOU WANT TO LEAVE TOWN

With some of South Africa's most dramatic topography slap bang in the middle of town, and golden sands aplenty, it is by no means essential to leave Cape Town for some R&R. However, for those who are willing to hop in a car and drive for an hour or two, there is adventure, wildlife and gastronomic delight in spades. Our three options are possible as day trips, but are better still with an overnight stay, or you could combine them as a three-day tour.

Although Kruger National Park is 18 hours from Cape Town, Aquila Safari (opposite), just 90 minutes from the city centre, will satisfy the urge to hit the bush for those who feel that a visit to the continent is incomplete without seeing some big game. Aquila will feel safari-lite to the experienced, but the sight of four out of the big five and an awesome setting will please most others.

A taste of the winelands can be had over lunch (see p042), but it's far better to book a night in the pretty town of Franschhoek (see p102), an hour from Cape Town, where many of the wineries can be explored on foot from the main street, and the choice of fine cuisine demands you stay for lunch and dinner. Lastly, while southern right whales can be seen from Cape Town, Hermanus, 90 minutes to the east, is the local whale-watching hub. The most comfy place to spot them is from a lounger on the terrace at the five-star, cliff-edge Birkenhead House Hotel (see p100).

For full addresses, see Resources.

Aquila Safari

Forget that there are fences around these 4,500 hectares of former sheep farm turned Karoo conservancy, and focus on the fact that you are in Africa, surrounded by zebras, wildebeest, springbok, rhinos and more. Sipping a glass of sparkling wine beside your jeep as the setting sun casts a glow on the mountains is a thrill that's hard to beat – unless you get up for a horseback safari the next morning.

Sleeping in a four-poster bed by a log fire, with little between you and the wildlife, is special too. The bathroom and sunken bath in Premier Luxury Chalet 8 (overleaf) are cut into the rock; Chalet 9 boasts a jacuzzi. Dinner, which is served by paraffin lamp, is basic but hearty.
T 021 421 4998, www.aquilasafari.com

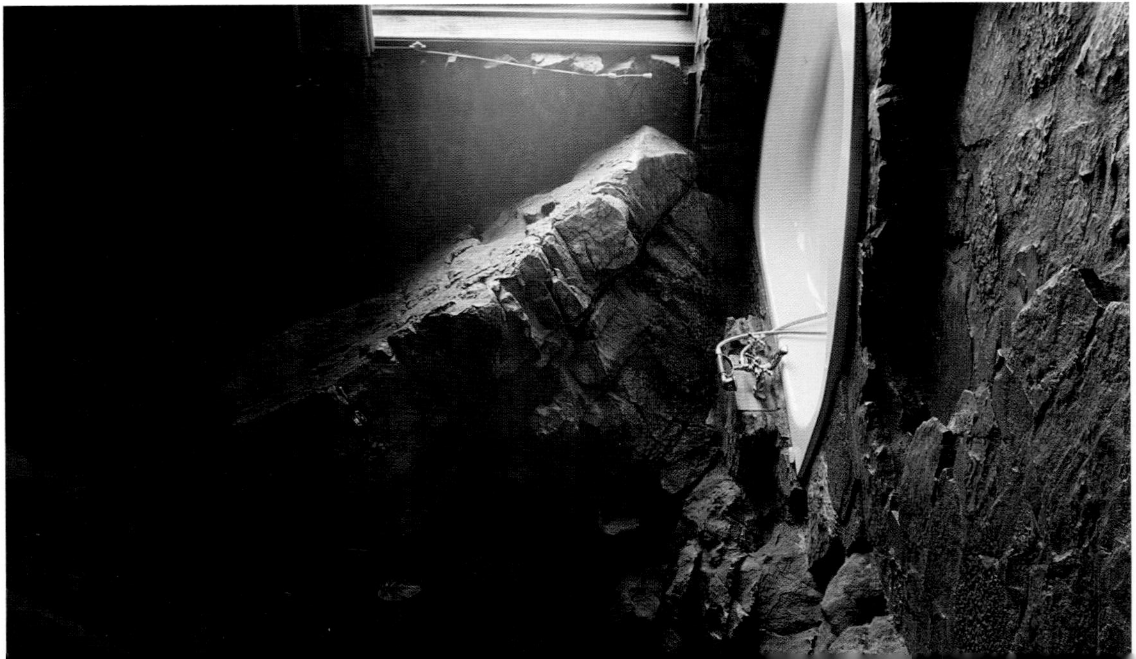

Birkenhead House Hotel, Hermanus

Whale watching is big business in this part of the world, where females come in shore to calve from July to October, and may be seen between May and December. But it doesn't have to be about cagoules and feeling queasy. Ignore the ugly sprawl of Hermanus town and make straight for the Birkenhead House Hotel, perched on a low cliff with a terrace and rim-flow pool (above), which looks out over the Indian Ocean. From here, or the opulent interiors (book Room 1 or 2 to ensure a view), you can see all the passing whales you wish, while looking your sophisticated self. For the return drive, take the scenic route, following the coast to Gordon's Bay, before getting back on the N2. Try to time it so that you pass Rooiels around sunset. *7th Avenue, Voëlklip, T 028 314 8000, www.birkenheadhouse.com*

Franschhoek Wine Valley
Offering the very best of the winelands'
sybaritic delights, a day in Franschhoek
allows time for tastings at La Motte for
reds (T 021 876 3119) and Cabrière for
fizz (T 021 876 2630). Stay in the five-
star Le Franschhoek Hotel (pictured)
and dine at its Le Verger restaurant.
*Le Franschhoek Hotel & Spa, Farm
Keerweder, Portion 22, Minor Road 16,
T 021 876 8900, www.lefranschhoek.co.za*

Dear Reader, Books by Phaidon are recognised world-wide for their beauty, scholarship and elegance. We invite you to return this card with your name and e-mail address so that we can keep you informed of our new publications, special offers and events. Alternatively, visit us at **www.phaidon.com** to see our entire list of books, videos and stationery. Register on-line to be included on our regular e-newsletters.

Subjects in which I have a special interest

☐ General Non-Fiction ☐ Art ☐ Photography ☐ Architecture ☐ Design

☐ Fashion ☐ Music ☐ Children's ☐ Food ☐ Travel

Mr/Miss/Ms   Initial   Surname

Name

No./Street

City

Post code/Zip code   Country

E-mail

This is not an order form. To order please contact Customer Services at the appropriate address overleaf.

Please delete address <u>not</u> required before mailing

PHAIDON PRESS INC.

180 Varick Street

New York

NY 10014

Return address for USA and Canada only

PHAIDON PRESS LIMITED

Regent's Wharf

All Saints Street

London N1 9PA

Return address for UK and countries
outside the USA and Canada only

*Affix
stamp
here*

NOTES

SKETCHES AND MEMOS

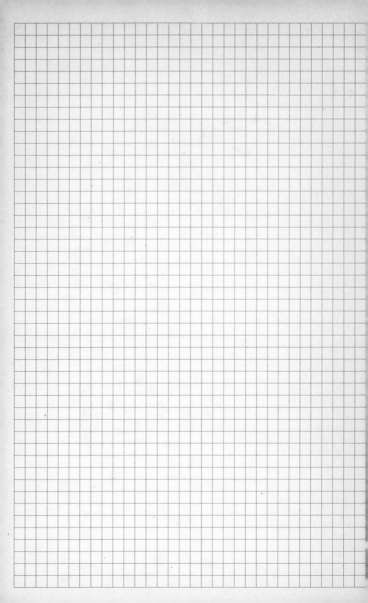

RESOURCES

CITY GUIDE DIRECTORY

HOTELS
ADDRESSES AND ROOM RATES

Alta Bay 020
Room rates:
double, R1,500-R2,100;
Bay Room, R1,500-R2,100
12 Invermark Crescent
T 021 487 8800
www.altabay.com

Daddy Long Legs 031
Room rates:
double, R490-R750;
Emergency Room, R490-R750;
The Freshroom, R490-R750;
The Photo Booth, R490-R750
134 Long Street
T 021 422 3074
www.daddylonglegs.co.za

Hippo Boutique Hotel 028
Room rates:
double, R1,300;
Standard Room, R1,300;
Room 105, R1,300
5-9 Park Road
T 021 423 2500
www.hippotique.co.za

Kensington Place 026
Room rates:
double, R1,400-R2,300;
Room 6, R1,400-R2,300;
Room 7 and Room 8, R1,700-R2,700
38 Kensington Crescent
T 021 424 4744
www.kensingtonplace.co.za

Lion's View 036
Room rates:
Penthouse, R3,300;
Main House, R8,000
4 First Crescent
T 021 438 1239
www.lionsview.co.za

Manolo Sleep 016
Room rates:
double, from R2,000
33 Leeukloof Drive
T 021 426 2330
www.manolosleep.co.za

Metropole 022
Room rates:
double, R1,190-R1,290;
Deluxe Suite 205, R1,890-R2,090
38 Long Street
T 021 424 7247
www.metropolehotel.co.za

Mount Nelson Hotel 034
Room rates:
double, R3,600-R5,925;
Garden Cottages, R7,230-R12,140
76 Orange Street
T 021 483 1000
www.mountnelson.co.za

On the Rocks 024
Room rates:
Apartment, R1,335-R4,722
Seacliffe Road
T 021 424 0905
www.icape.co.za

The Twelve Apostles 030
  Room rates:
  double, R4,450;
  Superior Room, R4,620;
  Suite 101, R8,150
  Victoria Road
  Oudekraal
  T 021 437 9000
  www.12apostleshotel.com
The Penthouse, Mutual Heights 017
  Room rates:
  Apartment, R3,750-R4,000
  Parliament Street/Darling Street
  T 021 794 3140
The Village Lodge 016
  Room rates:
  double, R600-R750
  49 Napier Street
  T 021 421 1106
  www.thevillagelodge.com

WALLPAPER* CITY GUIDES

Editorial Director
Richard Cook

Art Director
Loran Stosskopf
City Editor
Bridget Downing
Project Editor
Rachael Moloney
Executive Managing Editor
Jessica Firmin

Chief Designer
Ben Blossom
Designers
Ingvild Sandal
Dan Shrimpton

Map Illustrator
Russell Bell

Photography Editor
Christopher Lands
Photography Assistant
Jasmine Labeau

Chief Sub-Editor
Jeremy Case
Sub-Editor
Jane Mornement
Assistant Sub-Editor
Milly Nolan

**Wallpaper* Group
Editor-in-Chief**
Jeremy Langmead
Creative Director
Tony Chambers
Publishing Director
Fiona Dent

Contributors
Paul Barnes
Jeroen Bergmans
Alan Fletcher
Sara Henrichs
David McKendrick
Emma Moore
Claudia Perin
Meirion Pritchard
James Reid
Lloyd Smith
Ellie Stathaki

PHAIDON

Phaidon Press Limited
Regent's Wharf
All Saints Street
London N1 9PA

Phaidon Press Inc
180 Varick Street
New York, NY 10014
www.phaidon.com

First published 2007
© 2007 Phaidon
Press Limited

ISBN 978 0 7148 4720 7

A CIP Catalogue record
for this book is available
from the British Library.

All prices are correct at
time of going to press,
but are subject to change.

Printed in China

PHOTOGRAPHERS

Christopher Floyd
The Penthouse, Mutual Heights, p017
Metropole, p023
Birds Boutique Café, p053
La Perla, pp068-069
Bronwyn Davies, p071
Taal Monument, p073
Michael Stevenson Gallery, p081
Olive Green Cat, p084
Okha, p085
Sea Point Pavilion, pp090-091
Aquila Safari, p097, pp098-099

Jonathan de Villiers
Llandudno, pp044-045
Baxter Theatre Centre, pp074-075

David Southwood
Cape Town city view, inside front cover
Disa Park Towers, pp010-011
Table Mountain, p012
Rhodes Memorial, p013
Ritz Hotel, pp014-015
Mutual Heights, pp018-019
On The Rocks, pp024-025
Manna Epicure, p041
Tokara Wine Estate, pp042-043
Prins & Prins, p046
Manolo, p047
Newport Market & Deli, p049
Harbour House, pp050-051
Olympia Café and Deli, p052
Vida e Caffé, p054
95 Keerom, p055
Melissa's, pp056-057
Royal Eatery, p058
Capella, pp060-061
Guga S'Thebe Arts & Culture Centre, pp078-079
Hand, pp082-083
Newlands Cricket Ground, p089
Muizenburg, pp094-095

CAPE TOWN
A COLOUR-CODED GUIDE TO THE HOT 'HOODS

ATLANTIC SEABOARD
Modernist homes and discreet hotels nestle between the mountains and the beach

GREEN POINT
Rapidly gentrifying, the area is undergoing a major overhaul for the 2010 World Cup

CITY CENTRE
The city's nightlife hub with great bars and eateries, plus the haven of Company's Gardens

WATERFRONT
A slick shopping and entertainment centre, with a working marina, aimed at tourists

LOWER CITY CENTRE
Built on land reclaimed from the sea, this business district houses the city's high-rises

CITY BOWL SUBURBS
Upmarket restaurants, shops and boutique hotels are centred around Kloof Street

For a full description of each neighbourhood,
including the places you really must not miss, see the Introduction